GET *that* GRANT!

Grant Basics:
Before, During, and After Submitting the Proposal

by Dawn Costantiello

www.stepcraft.us info@stepcraft.us

GET THAT GRANT!

Get that Grant, Edition 1
By Dawn Costantiello

Written by: Dawn Costantiello
Cover Art: Michelle Spray
ISBN: 9781696413930

Get that Grant!

GET THAT GRANT!

INTRODUCTION

This book was written for every school, robotics team, and/or *education* focused nonprofit or community-based group pursuing grants to purchase equipment for their programs. As a former teacher, and president of a non-profit for over five years, I sympathize with and fully understand the struggles that budget limitations create for these types of organizations.

My primary goal was to create an easy-to-follow format, clear language guide to help simplify the complex process of grant writing. Whether you're a first time grant seeker or seasoned veteran, this step-by-step manual can make it more manageable and less stressful for all. Many of the concepts within these pages are not new, but were collected, tested, and then carefully renovated according to what worked for me (and what didn't) within twenty years of researching and writing grant applications.

My other goal with this book was to make the daunting task of finding and qualifying grant opportunities easier and less time-consuming for anyone interested. This is why I invested my time, on your behalf, researching and qualifying the wealth of funding opportunities at the end. There are thousands of viable grants, just waiting to be won, and each new print edition of this book will contain updated information and have new opportunities added. *Enjoy the read and good luck!*

Dawn Costantiello
Sales Manager & Education Specialist
STEPCRAFT, Inc. (USA)
dawn@stepcraft.us
(860) 866-4231

Why Should you apply for a grant?
Why NOT?!

Grants offer a chance for your organization to receive funds that do not need to be reimbursed, so your organization can expand into areas you may not have been able to otherwise. There is no limit to the number of grants any one organization can apply for each year, and that could add up to a lot of funding! Receiving a grant can also be prestigious, gaining exposure for your cause. The publicity can strengthen your standing within a community, and make future fundraising easier. Besides the money awards, there are other benefits to the grant process itself that you may not have realized...

- It sheds light on your organization and the mission you hold.
- It can lead to improvement within your existing program structure as you survey areas of need, inventory resources, and establish goals.
- It encourages change and growth, often leading to new or greatly improved initiatives.
- It is an excellent reason to network with similar organizations to yours, and collaborate. Strong partnerships can increase the success of all participants. There is strength in numbers!
- Even if funds are not awarded to your program, it is a true learning experience, and a chance to develop skills that will carry over into many other areas of your organization.

What is a Grant?

By textbook **definition,** a grant is "a sum of money given by a government or other organization for a particular purpose."

Wikipedia Explains:

"Grants are non-repayable funds or products disbursed or given by one party (grant makers), often a government department, corporation, foundation or trust, to a recipient, often (but not always) a nonprofit entity, educational institution, business or an individual. In order to receive a grant, some form of "Grant Writing" often referred to as either a proposal or an application is required.

Most grants are made to fund a specific project and require some level of compliance and reporting. The grant writing process involves an applicant submitting a proposal (or submission) to a potential funder, either on the applicant's own initiative or in response to a Request for Proposal from the funder. Other grants can be given to individuals, such as victims of natural disasters or individuals who seek to open a small business. Sometimes grant makers require grant seekers to have some form of tax-exempt status, be a registered nonprofit organization or a local government."

Get that Grant!

The Three Main Sources for Grant Funding

1. **Government** – usually state or federal, and occasionally local.
2. **Private businesses and corporations**
3. **Foundations** – distribute millions of dollars each year to community groups and organizations.

Grant Types

- A **federal grant** is awarded by a government agency to carry out a public purpose of support or to provide stimulation by law of the United States. These grants are not loans and are not federal assistance. They cannot be used to acquire property or to buy groceries.

- A **private grant** is given by a foundation, corporation, or non-governmental agency. These can be easier to get than federal grants, as private institutions are not buried under as much bureaucracy and red tape as the federal government.

- A **public charity grant** gives funds to charitable organizations: those having 501(c)3 status with the IRS.

Grant Classifications

- A **Categorical Formula Grant** is given for a specific purpose that has restrictions regarding how the money can be spent. There are two types:
    - **Project Grants:** Money states apply for by submitting specific project proposals
    - **Formula Grants:** Money given to states according to a mathematical formula
- A **Block Grant** is money given for a broad purpose with few strings attached

Plan Ahead

Give yourself enough time

If your program needs funding by a certain time then START EARLY. Don't apply for a grant with a November deadline if you need funds in December. Each new application, review, and approval process can take months, and then additional time to deliver money to the winner(s).

Consult an expert

Speak with someone familiar with grant applications for advice or assistance. Your organization, town, or state may have someone, or you may know someone without realizing it.

Do your homework

Carefully read the entire grant packet, list of requirements, and the rules you are expected to follow. Whatever they ask for, make sure you give them that, and only that! Make a list of anything unclear in the directions, and contact the Grant Administrator with those questions for clarification. Also ask who will be reviewing the application, and research their position and expertise. Customize the proposal, if possible within the guidelines, to their background. If your application is interesting to them personally, they will read it all and remember it!

Get that Grant!

Emulate a Successful Model

If you can acquire a previous grantee's application funded by your chosen foundation, then you will have a huge advantage. Find a list of past awardees to contact, explain your organization's goals, and politely request the information. Chances are you will have a lot in common with them and be involved in similar projects since they sought the same grant. Most will be happy to provide you with a proposal copy along with other tips and valuable insight. Once you have the written model, examine it carefully and use it as a reference tool. Did they use casual language or formal? How is it structured? Were there unique touches that made them stand out? How much documentation was included? Was the foundation more interested in numbers or the vision behind them? While you should never copy another's work verbatim, using those answered questions as a guide will help you match the style and structure a grantor prefers.

Create a Timeline

Working backward from the due date, create a list of important tasks that need to be completed. Record who will responsible for completing them, and assign a due date to each one. About half of your time will used researching and collecting data for your project, and the other half will be used writing the grant application including all that information. Use your time wisely!

AVOID COMMON MISTAKES

MAKE SURE YOU ARE ELIGIBLE

Before investing your valuable time, make sure that your organization and/or project meets the parameters of that specific grant application. Many applications are rejected simply because they don't "fit" the description.

THE APPLICATION MUST BE LEGIBLE

Writing by hand is acceptable IF the reader can understand it. It would be a shame to be overlookedfor messy penmanship after all that effort!

FOLLOW THE DIRECTIONS

Each foundation and/or granting agency has the right to do things uniquely. It is important that you study their specific guidelines and follow their rules completely. If they ask for 5 pages then submit ONLY 5 pages. If tax exempt status proof is requested then provide it. If they want resumes or letters of support added, then attach them. If they want a certain font used then use only that font. If they want a detailed budget outline then include it. If the submission deadline is January 1st then send your proposal in at least one full week BEFORE January 1st... and so on. Ignoring the rules will only count against you!

COVER LETTER OR NOT?

You know the saying "you only get one chance to make a first impression?" The cover letter test is yours. Creating a strong cover letter can place you in a good starting position in the mind of the grant reader. Some State and Federal Grantors do NOT want a cover letter and if you include one anyway it will likely land you at the bottom of the candidate pile with the other rule-breakers. All other grant makers, with written applications, require a cover letter. Some online applications do give you the option to upload one.

Get that Grant!

Less is more

Unless a grant foundation specifically states they will accept multiple copies of a proposal, do NOT send more than one. It is a common misconception that sending multiples may increase an organization's chances, this is false. Most foundations want only one submission, and flooding them can hurt your chances. It is best to find the main point of contact for the grant maker and send it only there. This reflects back on the importance of following their rules.

Check the math

Calculations should always be reviewed for errors before a proposal is officially submitted. If the application includes budgetary plans, or other financial information, then it should be double-checked by someone overseeing those matters for the organization. Math mistakes take time to sort out by the grantors and can hurt your chances of winning.

Contact information

Be clear who the contact person is for your organization, and make sure the phone number and email address provided for that person are correct. If the grant maker needs more information, it should not be hard to get in touch with the right person. If several people sign a letter, or are named in an application, it can be confusing and cause problematic delays.

WRITING YOUR PROPOSAL

COVER LETTERS

- Use your organization's letterhead
- Should be no longer than one page
- Address the letter to a specific person in charge, using their correct personal title
- Introduce your organization and express full support of the application by all members
- Describe how your application is in sync with the funder's requirements and goals.
- Briefly state what you are asking for (amount or items) and the reason.
- Do not repeat information that is the body of your proposal

POSITIVE WORDING

Keep it upbeat and highlight the exciting plans your program has for the grant money. Avoid negative writing like "If we don't get this money we won't be able to...:" etc. Show passion that grabs the reader, so they will want to follow the entire story to the end.

MAKE IT EASY

Highlight your point at the start of every section and at the end of each paragraph. Grant reviewers have numerous proposals to read, and this prepares yours for the "skimmers."

BE CONCISE

Use short, purposeful sentences and paragraphs. Edit multiple times, cutting out unnecessary words and redundant phrases. Grant readers have hundreds of applications to read, and they will appreciate this effort.

Get that Grant!

Use simple language

Write in such a way that anyone could understand what you are saying.
Avoid overly complex vocabulary and never use acronyms or slang.
Making grant readers work harder to comprehend what is written will
only be counterproductive. Clarity is key.

Be transparent

Don't leave grant makers to assume or choose how you would
use funds by describing several ways you COULD use it. Clearly
communicate a fixed plan for the funds you seek, and the direct
benefits it will provide to your organization and the community it
serves. Share any budget information necessary to effectively outline
your goals.

Make it personal

IF it is appropriate, personalizing your application with a few uplifting
short stories can "humanize" your organization and make the reviewer
more empathetic toward your goals. Remember that the grant makers
are investing in YOUR MEMBERS as much as the program's vision, so
you must market yourself.

Focus on the future

Emphasize what you intend to accomplish using the purchase(s) from
the grant money, rather than the actual items themselves. What
will evolve from the Grant awarded? Foundations prefer donating to
organizations who organize projects with a long-lasting impact.

(continued...)

Get that Grant!

Share the wealth
Grantors want their donations to be as far-reaching as possible. If
you can show how your project/program will benefit others in similar
organizations or the community, your proposal will grab their attention.
If your project/program can easily be replicated by others, thereby
benefiting even more people in the future, that can also increase your
chances of winning the funds.

Growing the Funds
Good grant applications become even more attractive when an
organization can show how they can use the money to secure even
more funding. Foundations want the best value for their dollars, and
for their awards to be used most effectively. Give examples like
"With the purchase of this equipment we will save money spent on
prototyping, which will then be used to secure a professional to train
additional volunteers that will head additional outreaches" and so forth.

Highlight your wins
It is a common misconception that grant makers may shy away from
awarding a grant to an organization who has already won other funding.
National foundations look for organizations strongly supported in
their communities. If they can show they have obtained other grants,
it is a plus. It indicates sustainability and the talent to create lasting
impressions.

Test it out
Once your proposal is ready, have someone not affiliated with your
organization read it. Determine if they understood the writing and
retained the message. Ask for specific feedback. If necessary, make
adjustments to the application to clarify your content.

Be patient
Grant makers get flooded with applications, so it takes time to
properly sort through them. It may take up to two months to receive a
confirmation of receipt, let alone a detailed response.

Get that Grant!

Get feedback

If your proposal gets rejected, contact the grant administrator to request a copy of the reviewer's comments. If those are not recorded, then ask if there is any constructive criticism available for you to evaluate. Was there one or several reasons for rejection? What was the strongest part? What was the weakest? How could the application be improved? Remember that once you have a strong proposal you can submit it again to many different funding opportunities with only minor changes tailored to the requirements of each one.

Catalog everything

Keep copies of all your research, ideas, written plans, and proposals! Every application has unique aspects, but there are also many similarities between them. Whether you seek several grants within the same year, or apply to the SAME opportunities each new year... Why start from scratch every time? Besides the time saving benefit of filing your work for future proposals, the fresh insight about your organization's current goals and evolving mission learned with every new application is priceless. Use these documented discoveries to strategize paths to new growth and keep your positive momentum moving forward.

Be thankful

If your application is funded, regardless of the amount, then writing a thank you note to the grantor is the first thing you should do. A proper thank you is a thoughtful hand-written message, on a real card, either mailed or personally delivered. Sadly, research shows that 70% of winning organizations neglect to extend this courtesy. Without acknowledgement, the funding party will wonder if they made the right decision, feeling you don't value the gift. They want to know you are grateful and excited about carrying out the vision they contributed to. Maintaining a good relationship with donors will also help your chances of receiving future funding from them. Remember to also thank anyone who helped you research/write the application!

Sample Thank you letter

(Date here)

Dear (Title and Name),

Thank you so much for your generous contribution to us at (name of organization) for (amount of grant). We are extremely grateful for your support to (program title) through your grant. The money will be used for (indicate some specific purchases).

This funding will be especially important to (people the program will benefit) by (one to two sentences of how it will make a lasting impact). We are very excited to get started!

Sincerely,

(Your signature)
(Your name - printed or typed)
(Your title - printed or typed)

NEVER GIVE UP

My best advice is to stay persistent and don't get discouraged!
You may obtain a grant with your first attempt, or it may take several...
By following the steps in this book you will shorten your path to success!

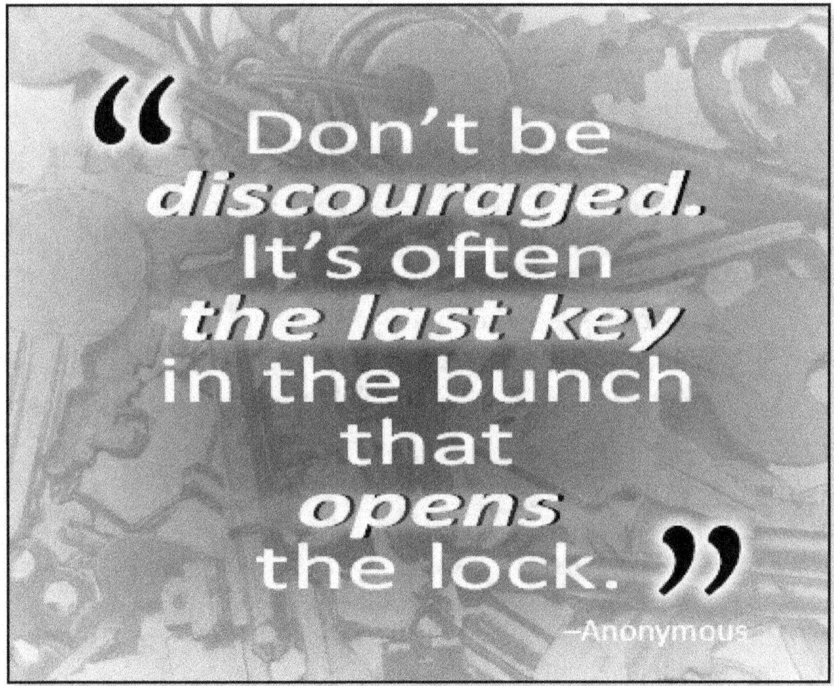

GET THAT GRANT!

EDUCATION FOCUSED GRANTS & FUNDING OPPORTUNITIES

KEY

AWESOME FOUNDATION GRANTS 

About Us. The Awesome Foundation is a global community advancing the interest of awesome in the universe, $1000 at a time. Each fully autonomous chapter supports awesome projects through micro-grants, usually given out monthly.

- Open to all educators of various types and levels
- Nationwide eligibilities
- up to $1,000. each
- Rolling Deadlines – year round
- Open to all education based groups

https://www.awesomefoundation.org/en/about_us

DOMINION GRANTS 

Grant applications are accepted online. Awards are made primarily in areas where Dominion Energy provides retail electricity or natural gas services or has significant facilities or business interests.

- Must be a 501(c) nonprofit organization
- Nationwide eligibilities
- Varied amounts between $1.000-$15,000 each
- Rolling Deadlines– year round

https://www.dominionenergy.com/company/community/dominion-energy-charitable-foundation/apply-for-a-grant

AMBROSE MONELL FOUNDATION GRANTS 

This Foundation has made a long-term commitment to voluntarily aiding and contributing to scientific, cultural, educational, and other charitable initiatives.

- Must be a 501(c) nonprofit organization
- Nationwide eligibility
- Varied amounts with average award of $25,000-$50,000
- Rolling deadlines – year round

http://www.monellfoundation.org

STEMGRANTS.COM GRANTS 

Over 100 grant opportunities for Colleges and Universities with STEM focused initiatives.

- Must be a College or University
- Nationwide eligibilities
- Varied amounts
- Rolling deadlines – year round

http://stemgrants.com/stem-grants-for-universities-and-colleges/

DIGITAL WISH GRANTS & FUNDING 

Over 100 grant links for Educators and 501(c) Non-Profit Organizations in areas of Math, Technology, and more! The Digital Wish site also allows you to create a profile for your school or classroom, and then anyone can make a donation toward your goals.
http://www.digitalwish.com/dw/digitalwish/grants

(continued...)

(continued...)

STEMfinity STEM Based Program Grants 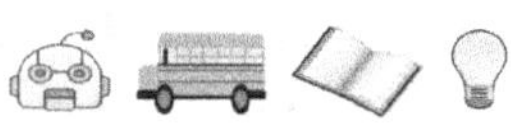

STEMfinity has over 1000 STEM grant opportunities for educational programs programs that further the arts, culture, education, science, and human services.
- Nationwide eligibilities
- Varied amounts
- Rolling deadlines – year round

https://www.stemfinity.com/STEM-Education-Grants

Get EdFunding Grants 

GetEdFunding hosts thousands of education grants, including funding opportunities for public and private preK–12 schools and districts; awards for outstanding professionals; grants for teachers, media specialists, and administrators; higher education institutions; and nonprofit organizations offering educational programs.
- Nationwide eligibilities
- Varied Amounts
- Rolling deadlines – year round

https://www.getedfunding.com/c/index.web?s@II5JjNzqcYK5o

Grants.gov Directory 

On this site organizations to electronically find and apply for thousands of competitive grant opportunities from all Federal grant-making agencies. Do not get scammed into paying "search fees" by other sites when this information is free!
http://www.grants.gov

Get that Grant!

AAUW Community Action Grants 

Community Action Grants provide funds to individuals, AAUW branches, and AAUW state organizations as well as local community-based nonprofit organizations for innovative programs or non-degree research projects that promote education and equity for women and girls. Special consideration is given to projects focused on K–12 and community college girls' and women's achievements in science, technology, engineering, or math.

- Must be an all girl organization
- Nationwide eligibility
- Varied amounts
- Open August 1st - December 1st each year

https://www.aauw.org/what-we-do/educational-funding-and-awards/community-action-grants/

The Paradigm Challenge Awards  

Participate in The Paradigm Challenge individually or as teams of any size. The Paradigm Challenge is an ongoing competition that invites students aged 4 to 18 around the world to use kindness, creativity, and collaboration to help solve real-life problems and make a difference.

- Open to students ages 4 to 18
- Nationwide eligibility
- Varied amounts – multiple winners receive over $100,000. total
- Deadline closes in May each year

https://www.projectparadigm.org/

(continued...)

GET THAT GRANT!

(continued...)

HONDA
THE POWER OF DREAMS GRANTS 
American Honda Foundation helps meet the needs of American society in the areas of youth and scientific education by awarding grants to nonprofits, while strategically assisting communities in deriving long-term benefits. The American Honda Foundation engages in grant making that reflects the basic tenets, beliefs and philosophies of Honda companies, which are characterized by the following qualities: imaginative, creative, youthful, forward-thinking, scientific, humanistic and innovative. We support youth education with a specific focus on the STEM (science, technology, engineering and mathematics) subjects in addition to the environment.

- All youth education programs of science, technology, job training +
- Must be a 501(c) nonprofit organization or private/public school
- Nationwide eligibility
- Awards range from $20,000-$75,000
- Various deadlines depending on "new or "returning" organization status

https://www.honda.com/community/applying-for-a-grant

FIRST ROBOTICS FRC ROOKIE TEAM GRANTS 
Community Action Grants provide funds to individuals, AAUW branches, and AAUW state organizations as well as local community-based nonprofit organizations for innovative programs or non-degree research projects that promote education and equity for women and girls. Special consideration is given to projects focused on K–12 and community college girls' and women's achievements in science, technology, engineering, or math.

- MUST be a FIRST Robotics FRC Rookie Team
- Nationwide eligibility
- Multiple winners
- Varied awards
- Submission deadline and announcement of winners date varies each year

https://www.firstinspires.org/robotics/frc/grants

QUESTIONS? frcgrants@firstinspires.org

FIRST Robotics FTC Rookie Team Grants 

Community Action Grants provide funds to individuals, AAUW branches, AAUW state organizations, and local community-based nonprofit organizations for innovative programs that promote education and equity for women and girls. Special consideration is given to projects focused on K–12 and community college girls' and women's achievements in science, technology, engineering, or math.

- Must be a FIRST Robotics FTC Rookie Team
- Nationwide eligibility
- Multiple winners
- $275. Registration fee grant, and $225. Product grant for FTC Storefront for supplies
- Submission deadline and announcement of winners date varies each year

https://usfirst.submittable.com/submit/6d35d136-4d6f-4645-8fc5-5483cdb2a941/2019-2020-first-tech-challenge-rookie-team-grant

QUESTIONS? ftcgrants@firstinspires.org

U.S. Department of Education Grants 

This site is a compilation of all federal grants, a description of the grant, requirements with filing deadlines, electronic filing forms, and the home page for each of the grants listed

- Must be a registered school
- Varied amounts
- Various deadlines – year round

http://www.ed.gov/GrantApps

(continued...)

(continued...)

SHELL GRANTS 

Shell makes educational grants to qualified nonprofit groups, with special consideration given to requests from organizations in or near communities in the United States where Shell Oil Company has a major presence. Grant requests related to education must focus on Shell's funding priorities. Funding is provided to support programs in kindergarten through Grade 12 that are designed to boost students' mathematics and science skills. At the university level, Shell supports programs that aid engineering and geoscience students and departments. Of particular interest are programs in mathematics, science, and technology that engage women/girls and minority students.

- Must be a 501(c) nonprofit organization, K-12 school, or University program
- Nationwide eligibility
- Varied amounts
- Rolling deadlines – year round

https://www.shell.us/sustainability/request-for-a-grant-from-shell.html#vanity-aHR0cHM6Ly93d3cuc2hlbGwudXMvZW52aXJvbm1lbnQtc29jaWV0eS9ncmFudC5odG1s

LOCKHEED MARTIN CONTRIBUTIONS 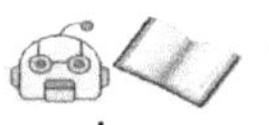

Lockheed Martin is committed to a program of philanthropy that supports the Corporation's strategic business goals, primarily in the focus areas of science, technology, engineering and mathematics (STEM) education and military and veteran causes. Lockheed Martin's philanthropic activities are administered by the communications representatives at the Corporation's operating units around the country and at corporate headquarters. In general, philanthropic contributions to national initiatives and organizations are made from corporate headquarters and contributions to local programs are made by Lockheed Martin sites close to the program.

Get that Grant!

- Must be a 501(c) nonprofit organization, public elementary/secondary school, or be a U.S. based institute of higher education.
- Awarded quarterly
- Varied amounts
- Rolling deadlines – year round

https://www.lockheedmartin.com/en-us/who-we-are/communities/applying-for-contributions.html

The Ford Family Foundation Grants & Scholarships

This Foundation has made a long-term commitment to voluntarily aiding and contributing to scientific, cultural, educational, and other charitable initiatives.

- Applicants/Organizations must be in Oregon or Siskiyou County, California
- Varied amounts with awards ranging from $1,000-$500,000
- Various deadlines – year round

https://www.tfff.org/how-we-work/grants/apply-grant

GrantsAlert Search

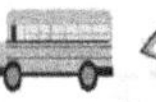

This site details multiple education and community related grants and allows you to search by alphabetical list, state, grant types (corporate, federal, foundation, and state), and date added. There are also articles about fundraising, writing grants, and more.

https://grantsalert.com

eSchool News Technology Funding

A comprehensive source for school technology funding. This website provides access to multiple grant opportunities, equipment donations, and Technology Funding Directory.

http://www.eschoolnews.com/funding

(continued...)

(continued...)

THE NATIONAL SCIENCE  FOUNDATION (NSF) GRANTS & FUNDING

The NSF funds research and education in science and engineering through grants, contracts, and cooperative agreements. The foundation accounts for about 20 percent of federal support to academic institutions for basic research. Through the links below you will find thousands of available grants and funding opportunities!

- Nationwide eligibilities
- Varied amounts
- Various deadlines - year round

http://www.nsf.gov/funding   *listed by category*
http://www.nsf.gov/funding/azindex.jsp   *listed by name*

GRANTSFORTEACHERS SEARCH 

Free resource for K-12 teachers. Extensive collection of over 100 grant opportunities!
https://grantsalert.com

DONORSCHOOSE.ORG FUNDRAISING

Are you a public school teacher in need of funding? Supporting teachers and students since 2000, DonorsChoose.org makes it easy for anyone to help a classroom in need. Public school teachers from every corner of America create classroom project requests, and donors can give any amount to the project that inspires them.
http://www.donorschoose.org

GOFUNDME.COM FUNDRAISING

Create a custom on-line fundraiser for your team, school, or community organization.
http://www.gofundme.com

Get that Grant!

VEX Robotics Rookie Team Grants 

Through the generosity of our sponsors, the REC Foundation Team Grant Program seeks to match schools and organizations that are interested in adopting the world's largest and fastest growing academic robotics competitions with the program resources necessary to get started. These grants are intended for schools and organizations that are not currently participating in one of our programs: VEX IQ Challenge, VEX Robotics Competition (VRC), and VEX U. VEX IQ Challenge grants are for elementary and middle schools (grades 3-8). VRC grants are for middle and high schools (grades 6-12).

- MUST be a NEW VEX Robotics Team
- Nationwide eligibility
- Multiple awards
- Submission deadline and announcement of winners date varies each year

https://www.roboticseducation.org/competition-teams/team-grants/

QUESTIONS? support@robotevents.com

Walmart Community Grants  

"Walmart believes in operating globally and giving back locally – creating impact in the neighborhoods where we live and work. The Community Grant Program proudly provides funding to local organizations."

- Must be either a 501(c) nonprofit organization, a recognized government entity: state, county, or city agency, or K-12 public or nonprofit private school, charter school, community/ junior college, state/private college or university, or faith based organization with a proposed project that benefits the community at large.
- Nationwide eligibility
- Multiple awards between $250-$5,000 each
- Grant cycle open from February to December each year
- Organizations may only submit a total number of 25 applications and/or receive up to 25 grants within one grant cycle.

https://walmart.org/how-we-give/local-community-grants

(continued...)

CORNING INC. FOUNDATION GRANTS 

Through its focus on education, human services, and volunteerism, the Corning Foundation collaborates with nonprofit organizations to foster and sustain communities.

- Should be a Nonprofit or School
- Program must impact people within a 20-mile radius of one of
- the many 50+ employee businesses Corning has in the United
- States (map on website)
- Multiple awards
- Various grant cycles

http://www.corningfoundation.org/how-we-give/how-we-give-grants

STEPCRAFT – EDUCATION GRANTS   EDU

STEPCRAFT is an international market leader in the world of multi-functional CNC systems. With our numerous unique attachment options, STEPCRAFT makes Sole Source products that bear the "Made in Germany" quality seal. STEPCRAFT currently offers both D-Series (desktop) Machines, and Q-Series (production) Machines in a total of 7 different sizes.

- Should be a Robotics team, school, or other Educational Program
- Must have an active social media presence on Instagram, Twitter, and Facebook
- USA and Canada eligible
- Varied amounts with awards ranging from $250.00 up to $2500.00
- Grants awarded in the form of STEPCRAFT USA Store Credit to purchase STEPCRAFT CNC products
- Rolling deadlines – year round
- Online application
- Standard EDU discount available to applicants not awarded

http://www.stepcraft.us/grantinformation

Get that Grant!

Follow STEPCRAFT on Social Media!

Facebook Group: www.facebook.com/groups/stepcraftforeducation

Facebook Page: www.facebook.com/STEPCRAFTforEDU

Twitter: www.twitter.com/stepcraftforedu

Instagram: www.instagram.com/stepcraftforedu

Pinterest: www.pinterest.com/stepcraftinc/stepcraft-for-education

Facebook: www.facebook.com/stepcraftinc
Twitter: www.twitter.com/stepcraftinc
Instagram: www.instagram.com/stepcraftusa
Pinterest: www.pinterest.com/stepcraftinc

YouTube: www.youtube.com/stepcraftinc

Notes

Notes

Notes

Notes

Notes

Notes

Notes

All Grant information
is verified
and updated
before each new
print edition
of this book.